100 Must Do

Philippines

TOP-10 Islands

Outdoor Adventures, Best Beaches, Hotels and Hostels, Eat & Drink, Historical and Cultural Sights, Advice of Local people, Souvenirs

by Kevin Hampton

Copyright 2018 by Kevin Hampton - All rights reserved.

All rights Reserved. No part of this publication or the information in it may be quoted from or reproduced in any form by means such as printing, scanning, photocopying or otherwise without prior written permission of the copyright holder.

Disclaimer and Terms of Use: Effort has been made to ensure that the information in this book is accurate and complete, however, the author and the publisher do not warrant the accuracy of the information, text, and graphics contained within the book due to the rapidly changing nature of science, research, known and unknown facts and the internet. The Author and the publisher do not hold any responsibility for errors, omissions or contrary interpretation of the subject matter herein. This book is presented solely for motivational and informational purposes only.

Table of Contents

Mactan 5

Boracay 12

Panglao Island, Bohol 17

Coron Island 24

Siargao 30

One Hundred Islands 37

The Calamian Group of Islands 42

Gigantes Group of Islands, Panay 47

Caramoan Peninsula 51

Mindoro 56

Introduction

The Philippines is composed of 7100 islands of active volcanoes, green rice fields, megacities, pristine and talcum-powder white sand beaches, spectacular views, historical buildings, megacities, and happy people. The country is the perfect destination for tourists who want an island-hopping experience that takes them from one amazing panorama to the next one.

While the beaches are the things that attract visitors to the Philippines, there's plenty of room for sporty buffs that are into kayaking, water surfing, kiteboarding, mountain biking, trekking, and cayoneering. Ziplining has recently become a popular activity and, it should be noted that the country is, unofficially, known as the world's zipline capital.

Spontaneous travel plans are the best to go for when in the Philippines. The domestic fares are cheap and exciting. Last-minute travel plans as a way of migrating to good climate parts of the country are the fun things you can enjoy only in the Philippines.

With this said, what does the Philippines have to make it your dream vacation destination from the rest of the world? Let's explore!

The Philippines is one of the premiere countries to visit not only for its magnificent views but also for its warm and hospitable people. As the tourism slogan goes, «its more fun in the Philippines», and it definitely is!

Mactan

Mactan is actually the first place you land if you're planning to visit Cebu. The international airport is located in Mactan, connected by two bridges to Cebu City. The island is a popular weekend getaway from visitors coming from Korea, Manila, and Hong Kong. One of the topmost attractions with Cebu and Mactan are the island-hopping trips. The island of Mactan has much to offer visitors. Here are 10 incredible things you can enjoy on a visit to Mactan, Cebu.

Places TO STAY

Shangri-La Mactan Resort

For $260 per night, the 5-star Shangri-La Mactan Resort can be an ideal home away from home. Crystal blue waters, lush tropical gardens, two outdoor pools, a spa, and close proximity to the Mactan International Airport are just some of the benefits gained from the stay.

Amaris Bed and Breakfast, Lapu-Lapu

For less than $50 a night, Amaris B&B is your best bet when budget is the issue. The 3-star rating of the hotel is actually good for the affordable price. Other amenities include free Wi-Fi a private terrace for every room, daily housekeeping, and close proximity to the Mactan International Airport.

TO VISIT

Swim with the whale sharks *special mission!*

Swimming with the whale sharks is a thrilling and memorable activity offered only in Oslob, a neighboring island of Mactan. The whale sharks may look huge and scary but they are actually gentle creatures. Bus fare going to Oslob is about 160 PHP per person. A fee of 500 PHP covers whale shark watching on a hired boat. Additional payment of 500 PHP when you want to snorkel or swim with the whales.

Drop by Plantation Bay Resort

Plantation Bay Resort is a pricey and high-end hotel but open for public visits and viewing. The resort is a must-see. The stunning views of scenic sights such as the manmade beachfront make the visit worth the time and effort. The resort is only a 36-minute ride away from the Mactan International Airport and, surprisingly, costs less than Shangri-La Mactan Hotel.

Explore the island on a tricycle

Enjoy the sights and explore the island on board a tricycle. A tricycle is a motorcycle with an attached sidecar which locals use as their daily means of transportation. If you want a budget tour, tricycle tours are the best options. Tricycle tours are reliable, inexpensive, and one of the best ways to know more about the local color of Mactan.

Snorkeling, swimming, and diving in Moalboal

The countless white sand and coral-rich beaches in Mactan make it an ideal place for activities such as snorkeling, swimming, and diving. The beaches also teem with exotic fish species that are truly sights to behold. The very popular Moalboal Island Paradise is a 2 ½ hour drive away from Mactan International Airport. There are several options to take to reach Moalboal. You can hire a motorbike, a van, a taxi or on a public bus. Taxis and vans can cost around 3000 PHP.

Island hopping tour

Nothing can be more fun and exciting than an island hopping tour. Visiting various islands all in a day is one of the popular tourist activities in Mactan. The islands that can be included in the itinerary are Bantayan Island, Cebu Island, Sumilion Island, Malapascua Island, and a lot more. The boat hire, island entrance fees, and meals depend on the number of people and the choice of islands. For example, a single person island hopping tour costs around 5,500 PHP while a party of four people costs around 2,600 PHP per head.

Guitar Factory visit *Special mission!*

Mactan is famous as makers of the finest guitars. Visiting a guitar factory is a must-experience as a way to know how guitars are made. The presentation of different types, colors, sizes, designs, and shapes of guitars is a memorable experience for everyone. Buying a guitar from the factory is a smarter and cheaper option. It may only cost you 1,600 PHP while buying it from a mall or somewhere else could cost 2,100 PHP.

Include Cebu Happy World Museum

Quirky and delightful are some of the words used to describe Cebu Happy World Museum, a quick 11-minute trip from Mactan. It is aptly named for the museum is designed as a castle features 3D photos you can use as background for your selfies. Entrance fee for adults is 400 PHP and kids for 300 PHP.

Take time to visit the Lapu-Lapu Shrine

Mactan is also known as Lapu-Lapu City which makes visiting the shrine a must-do. Lapu-Lapu is a national Filipino hero that achieved fame as the one who killed the famous Spanish explorer, Magellan. The shrine is only a 21-minute taxi ride away from Mactan International Airport.

TO TASTE

Experience eating lechon

Lechon or roast pork is one of the food delicacies Mactan is famous for. The crunchy skin and the tender pork meat are culinary delights to enjoy and experience on a visit to the island. A kilo of lechon costs around 640 PHP.

Boracay

The 5km White Beach sands of Boracay can be a mind-blowing experience for a first-time visitor. Boracay has been known to be the Philippines' crown jewel when it comes to beaches. The recent surge of popularity has encouraged big developments in Boracay, turning it into one huge beach party all the time. Yet, compared to other Asian beach luminaries, Boracay has retained its mellow tone and ambiance. Here are ten travel tips to know to make your visit to Boracay an enjoyable and memorable one.

Travel tips

- A plane ride via Caticlan to Boracay is the quickest and most convenient way. However, it could also be expensive. Another alternative is a plane ride to Kalibo. It is a cheaper way but it will also cost you long hours of road travel.
- Going on a RoRo boat ride to Caticlan is a lesser known route. A free meal is included in this RoRo Ferry boat ride that can be an adventure by itself. This is the best option to take if you're not in a particular hurry and if budget is the issue.

Places TO STAY

Luxury hotels

The party vibe in Boracay can be exhausting and demanding. Quiet places are the best ways to escape a long day of partying. If budget is not the issue, five-star hotels that are secluded from the maddening crowd yet located in key areas is the perfect option to take. The Alta Vista de Boracay is a plush hotel that provides the perfect getaway from the crowd. It is a bit pricey at 2,500 Philippine Peso a night, but the amenities more than make up for it.

Budget Hotels

There are countless budget hotels that provide all the amenities for your stay without breaking the bank. One of this is Patio Pacific Boracay. A stay in the hotel gives you affordable rooms, free breakfast, and free airport transfers.

TO VISIT

Activities to take part in

- Obviously, swimming is the top activity offered in Boracay. Just remember to swim in areas with conspicuous lifeguards and only do it between the Red and Yellow flags if you're not a strong swimmer.
- Diving and snorkeling are activities that top the list in Boracay. Make it a monitored activity as a way to help stop the decline of coral cover.
- Simply lolling around and being lazy all day long is allowed and encouraged in the island. It's vacation time, remember?
- Hiking to other beach areas. Meeting the Ati tribe during a hiking trip can amaze you with their expert flora and fauna knowledge.
- Skydiving is for the adventurous. If you fall into this category, expect to have the time of your life in Boracay.
- Indulge in the party vibe all day and all night.

Follow Rules and regulations

- Children begging on the streets are one of the unfortunate truths in Boracay. The best thing to deal with them is not to give them money. Instead, give drinks or food and report them to the authorities.
- The Philippines does not allow prostitution. One way of avoiding a long trial and prison sentence is to steer clear from them. The prison conditions in the country are far from ideal.
- Hotel towels and bed sheets ruined by Henna tattoo inks will be automatically charged to your account. One way to avoid this is to give ample time for the tattoo ink to dry before you sleep or take a shower.
- Smoking is not allowed on the beach front. Imprisonment or a fine of Php 1,000 is levied on violators. There are designated areas on the beach paths for smoking.

Other tourist attractions in Boracay

Motag Living Museum is unlike no other. Experience living in the past before Boracay became what it is now by visiting this highly unusual and unique museum. Experience rice-planting, riding the tamaraw or dancing the Tinikling, national dance of the Philippines real-time on this museum.

Ariel's Point

A stone throw away from Boracay is an island known as Ariel's Point. Enjoy the fantastic scenery on your boat ride to the island. Make it extra thrilling and exciting by diving off the island's cliff platforms. Take your pick from heights ranging from 3 meters to 13 meters.

Visit nearby beaches

The White Beach is not the only beach in Boracay. There are other beaches that are must-sees such as Diniwid Beach, Ilig-Iligan Beach, Puka Beach, and Bulabog Beach. Each of these beaches has their own charming qualities and has the same white sands as well.

Must-see *Special mission!*

Willy's Rock is an interesting, controversial, and popular landmark sitting at the edge of boat station 1. It is considered as the most photographed attraction of the island. It is a volcanic rock with a Virgin Mary grotto on one side.

A Fascinating thing to experience

The Boracay sunset is one of the iconic experiences to have on the island. It is amazing, incredible, and memorable. Willy's Rock wins hands down as the best area to watch the sun set in this paradise island.

Only in Boracay

There are some things that you can only see and experience in Boracay. The Ocean View of Boracay distinguishes it from any other beach front in the world. The seemingly endless stretch of white sands with the incredible contrast of turquoise waters is one of the best views in the world.

TO TASTE

The culinary scene in Boracay is as vibrant as the place. The amazing cuisines served cater to all food tastes and preferences. Here are some of the culinary delights this beach island has to offer:

The freshest seafood

The freshest seafood is found in Boracay's wet markets, with D'Talipapa as the most popular one. A visit to the place guarantees freshly caught offerings of the day from squids, crabs, fish, prawns, and lobsters. Haggling is allowed and expected. Nearby restaurants can cook the seafood of your choice for a small charge.

Exotic Indian cuisine

True Food is a restaurant that serves authentic Indian cuisine. The Indian music background and the décor make the ambiance more genuine.

Panglao Island, Bohol

Alona Beach is the famous resort that is generally associated with Panglao Island. It is because of the vibrant nightlife especially during the weekends when locals check out the place and join in the fun with Korean and European visitors. Here are the top 10 tips and guidelines to make you enjoy your vacation to the hilt in Panglao Island, Bohol.

Travel tips

There are numerous ways to get to Panglao Island. If you happen to be in Cebu, taking the Fast Ferry is the best option. A plane ride from Manila to Bohol is another option. You can book an airport or pier pickup from your chosen resort in Panglao Island or from a travel agency.

Places TO STAY

Alona Northland Resort

The amenities of the 3.5 star Alona Beach Resort include free airport transfers, daily housekeeping, located at the heart of Panglao, and only a 310-meter distance from the white sand beach. A bit pricey at about 3,350 PHP per night, the hotel makes up for it by being one of the best around.

Moon Fools Hostel

Clean rooms, close proximity to the beach, free WiFi, and, best of all, affordable price are the things you enjoy in Moon Fools Hostel in Panglao. For 1,250 PHP a night you get to enjoy all these amenities during your stay in Panglao.

TO VISIT

Island hopping galore

Island hopping is taken to a higher level in Panglao Island. There's the chance to catch sight of dolphins during the boat ride. Island hopping rates depend on number of people and the time of the year. Usually the expected rates range from 1,200 to 1,800 PHP. There's snorkeling in Balicasag Island. You have to bring your own snorkel gear or get charged an extra 250 PHP for hiring one. If you want to check out Balicasag Island, you need to fork out an additional charge of 400 PHP per person.

Scuba Diving Packages *Special mission!*

Bohol teems with coral reefs and exotic aquatic species and the only way to enjoy them is to go scuba diving. There are scuba diving packages that are tailor-made for diving enthusiasts. A 26,000 PHP Scuba Diving Package per person includes:

- Free transfers from the Seaport or Airport
- Superior Room accommodation for 4 nights
- Free breakfast at Linaw Beach Resort
- 6 dives overall stretched over 2 days including packed lunch, use of equipment, and marine park fees
- All included eco-tour package (air-conditioned car, guide, lunch, and fees)

- Free body massage using the traditional "hilot" technique

Visit Bohol Bee Farm

Yearning for a real organic meal? Bohol Bee Farm is the perfect place to enjoy organic delights such as stir-fried seafood and veggies and soups and salads that are guaranteed fresh all the time. The food prices are affordable such as a Cassava Lasagna for 240 PHP or your choice of Ice Cream flavor at 50 PHP per scoop. It can be a healthy stopover option before you proceed to Panglao Resort.

Include a visit to the Chocolate Hills

Plan a side trip to marvel at the sight of the iconic landmark of Bohol, the chocolate hills. The incredible sight of seemingly countless chocolate hills is something that should not be missed while in Bohol. There are a lot of ways to get to chocolate hills from Panglao. Hiring a motorbike is one and another is a Bohol van tour that includes visiting other places other than the chocolate hills. Hiring a van for a day tour of Bohol could cost around 3,000 to 3,500 PHP.

Experience crossing the Loboc River Bridge
Special mission!

The bamboo bridge over Loboc River is a popular landmark in Bohol. The manmade bamboo bridge may look frail but it is an engineering feat to ensure safety for all those who dare to cross. This can be included in the day tour itinerary.

Tarsier watching

Watch the Tarsiers in their natural habitat. They are given the freedom to move anywhere they want to be or even to leave the sanctuary altogether. For a small entrance fee of 60 PHP per person, the chance to see a tarsier is a must-do in Panglao. Choosing the van tour for about 3,000 PHP includes a visit to the Tarsier sanctuary.

"Life's a beach"

Panglao Island is a place of neighboring beaches which makes it imperative to discover most of them during the visit. One of the best ways to do this is to make it a point to eat or drink at the different restaurants each resort has.

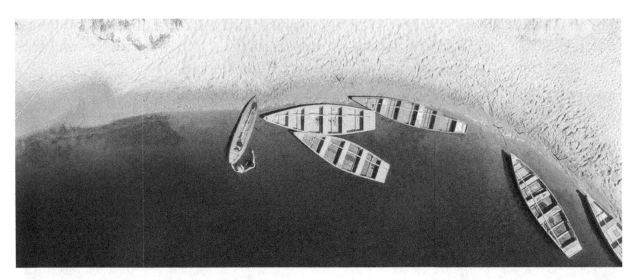

TO TASTE

Buzz Café

The Hungry Meh breakfast buffet of muffins, ham, waffle, pineapple juice, scrambled egg, and squash bread with spread cost an affordable 260 PHP.

Linaw Beach Resort & Pearl Restaurant

Watch the sunset as you enjoy a scrumptious dinner at Linaw Beach Resort & Pearl Restaurant. The wide range of culinary options from Western to Asian specialties makes the dinner choice a tough decision.

Coron Island

Mention Palawan and chances are people will give you 3 names: El Nido, Puerto Princesa, and Coron. Coron is a separate island and part of Busuanga, the biggest island of the Calamian Group of Islands. Stupendous views and marvelous beaches perfect for diving and snorkeling are the things to experience and enjoy in Coron. You can fly direct to Busuanga from Clark, Manila and Cebu. Mini vans can be hired in Busuanga to get you to the town of Coron. You can also opt for sea travel that directly takes you to Coron from Manila. Here are 10 things guaranteed to heat up a Coron vacation.

Places TO STAY

Two Seasons Coron Bayside Hotel

The price rate of 7,000 PHP per night makes this newest hotel addition to Coron the priciest of all. It has become one of the island's bestsellers because of the relaxing ambiance and good staff service.

Zuric Pension House

It's small, it's clean, it is right in the center of the town, and it's cheap. For 1,429 per night, Zuric is the perfect temporary home for a few days visit in Coron.

TO VISIT

View from the top of Kayangan Lake

The most iconic photo of Coron is usually of Kayangan Lake. The spectacular view of the cleanest lake in the Philippines is something that must be seen from the top. It's free. All you need to experience the magnificent view is a good pair of strong legs, stamina, and energy to climb the high craggy rocks surrounding Coron.

Island hopping tours

Island hopping tours are one of the most fun things to do in Coron. The main highlights of the tour include incredible views of the Twin Lagoon and Kayangan Lake. Hiring a boat to travel to these islands can set you back for a couple of thousand pesos. Not to worry, for there are Budget Island hopping tours for as little as 1,200 PHP. Visiting other islands such as Banana, Bulog, and Malcapuya cost an additional 1,200 PHP. Meals and entrance fees are not included.

Wreck diving

The wreck diving sites in Coron are world-class. Impressive wrecks of Japanese Supply boats pepper the diving sites, making it a thrilling and adventurous activity for the brave and adventuresome. Some of the wrecks are huge at 160 meters and some are in so deep. Hiring a professional is a must for this activity. Diving tours are more expensive at 17,500 PHP if you need to complete a diving course. If you're already certified the rate comes down to 3,000 PHP for two fun dives.

Relax in Maquinit Hot Springs

special mission!

Reputed to be one of the very few natural saltwater springs worldwide, Maquinit Hot Springs is a must-do in Coron. Take your pick from two smaller pools or the main pool. You can take a 30-minute tricycle ride to get to Maquinit. Hiring the tricycle costs about 300 PHP which is a pretty good deal as it will also take you back to Coron after your dip. Entrance fee is around 150 PHP.

Package dinner and firefly watch tour

Gastronomic delights are in store for you if you opt for the Panget package tour of dinner and firefly watch. Watching the fireflies while enjoying a buffet dinner in the floating restaurant is a one-of-a-kind lifetime experience. The buffet is a scrumptious serve of fresh seafood like crabs, fish, and more. The whole package costs between 950 to 1,000 PHP.

A motorcycle ride to the Calauit Safari Park

Calauit Safari Park is a game preserve in Coron where zebras and giraffes are allowed to roam free. The park is a 70 km distance from Coron that can be reached by motorcycle. Hiring a motorbike cost about $8.20 per day. There are several rent-a-motorcycle shops in Coron. Take time to read the online reviews before picking the shop you can rely on.

Take time to visit Culion Island

Culion Island was once the leper colony of the Philippines and considered as one the largest in the world. The World Health Organization declared the island leprosy-free in 2006. It is one must-see historical site when you're in Coron. The distance from Coron to Culion is 36.4 kilometers. A boat in the port of Coron leaves daily for Culion. The fare is around 180 PHP and the boat usually leaves at noontime. The return trip from Culion to Coron leaves at 7AM daily. Chartering a boat to sail to Culion is another option. A boat that can accommodate up to 4 passengers cost around 3,850 PHP.

Take a bicycle ride around town

Find out more about Coron town and the neighboring places by going for a mountain bike tour. There are bike tour packages that take you to all the nooks and crannies of Coron. However, if you just want a simple bike trip to discover local color, renting one for 500 PHP a day is one way to spend a vacation in Coron on a budget.

TO TASTE

Fika Café

The freshly baked goodies, free WiFi, and affordable price makes this café one of the favorites of tourists. The coffee is great too which makes it doubly important to check out the place.

Levine's Restaurant

Unwind after a busy day of adventuring in this rooftop bar and restaurant. Admire the magnificent view of the sunset as you enjoy a cold beer. Some of the best foods are in this place so make sure not to miss it.

Kuridas Bar

Head out to Kuridas Bar if you want a taste of the nightlife Coron has to offer. Rasta beats pumped out by the live band make things interesting. The unique layout of the bar and the great crowd make the bar one of the must-experience in Coron.

Siargao

Located at the easternmost part of the Philippines, Siargao is an island that became popular when John Callahan, famous surfing photographer, took pictures during the 90s. Since then, tourism has leveled up in this once sleepy island that boasts of tidal pools, big waves perfect for surfing, and clear waters. Here are the top ten tips to rely on when planning a vacation in Siargao.

Travel tips

You can take a direct flight from Cebu. The flight lands in Surigao City where you board a ferry boat for Siargao. Ferry rates cost about 250 PHP per head. Or you can fly direct to Sayak Airport from Manila. Sayak Airport is a 45-minute ride away from the tourist attractions of General Luna. Vans costing around 150 PHP per head and tricycles costing around 500 PHP for four people are the means of transportation to General Luna.

Places TO STAY

Malayah Siargao

Malayah Siargao hits the perfect spot for an adventuresome and lone traveler on a shoestring budget. The resort is a dormitory-type of lodging and renting out a bed only costs 450 PHP per night. The rooms are fully air-conditioned and a bit close to the main road.

Kubo Siargao Homestay *Special mission!*

Located in General Luna, this affordable hostel is like no other. For 1,300 a night, you get to temporarily own a private haven of 333 square meters complete with a working kitchen and a detached extra room.

Kalinaw Resort Siargao

A luxury resort that lives up to its reputation is Kalinaw Resort Siargao. Located in Catangnan, General Luna, it's a remote spot perfect for privacy and relaxation. For 12,900 a night, you get the luxury of having your own huge balcony lounge, private infinity pool, king-size bed, a hot tub, and a magnificent view of a lagoon.

TO VISIT

Island Hopping tours

It won't be a complete Siargao experience if island hopping is omitted. The must-see and must-experienced islands are Naked Island, Daku Island, and Guyam Island. Hiring a Bangka for 1,500 PHP that can accommodate four to six people is a fantastic deal. However, for lone female travelers, paying 1,000 PHP for shared island hopping rides is a safer option. Another thing, for 1000 PHP you get a free rental hut, guides to prepare and cook the food, and an almost endless supply of water, liquor, and sodas.

Traveling the islands gives plenty of opportunities for visitors to snorkel and swim. Hiring your own Bangka means swimming and snorkeling all you want. Going with a group means little time spending on the various islands.

Conquering the waves of Siargao

The single and most popular attraction of Siargao is their big waves, making it the Mecca capital of the country. Surfers from around the country and the world have always tried their luck in conquering the waves of the island.

A Bangka is the means of transport to reach the offshore breaks. Hiring a Bangka could be expensive at 1,500 PHP. Waiting for other surfers to share the ride is a better option. Sharing a Bangka ride with other surfers only cost around $5. The Bangka comes with its own "captain" which will wait for you or even go surfing with you if you need company. Don't be surprised if you find out that your "captain" is only 15 years old!

Taking a dip in the Tayangban Cave Pool
Special mission!

Clear waters from the Tayangban Cave Pool are a great way to combine cave exploration along with a cooling midday dip. The cave is an off-the-beaten track attraction that needs to be seen and experienced. Hiring a motorbike for 350-500 PHP is the best option to get to Tayangban Cave Pool. The pool is a 30-minute ride away from General Luna. Entrance fee is 70 PHP per head and you need to hire a guide for a tip fee of 100 PHP. The fees you pay include looking after your valuables while you are in the cave.

Expect a dark cave with some torches to light up the way. The water is not deep and swimming in the dark with an occasional bat flying over you can be a surreal and unique experience.

Cliff jumping in Magpupungko Tidal Pool

Non-surfers can have an adventurous experience by cliff jumping or swimming in the clear waters of Magpupungko Tidal Pool. Plan the visit to coincide with low tide hours to maximize the experience. Going there can be included with the trip to Tayangban Cave Pools. It's only a 10-minute ride away from Tayangban to Magpupungko. Hiring a tricycle to take you to both Magpupungko and the Tidal pools cost about 800 PHP. Entrance fee is 50 PHP per head.

Enjoy a cold douse in Taktak Falls

Siargao has only one waterfall, but, going for a cold shower beneath it is an exhilarating experience. The pure spring water cascading down on you makes this attraction a must-do in Siargao. It is a 1.5-hour scenic drive from General Luna to Taktak Falls. The best way is to hire a motorbike for around 500-800 PHP to get to the place. Entrance fee is 25 PHP per head. Bring your own food though there's a bakery in the area that sells "Pan de Surf", a delicious native bun.

Visit the natural habitat of the stingless Brown jellyfish

The Tojoman Lagoon is a must-see sight in Siargao. Home to the stingless brown jellyfish, the lagoon has become their sanctuary. You can swim with the jellyfishes without being stung by them. Just remember not to fish them out of the water for they will die. It is a 3-hour Bangka ride to Tojoman from General Luna. Hiring a Bangka for 4,000 PHP could be quite expensive for one or two travelers. If you go with this, make it more worthwhile by taking a side trip visit to Sohoton and Makukuob Caves.

Cloud 9 Experience

The most iconic landmark in Siargao is probably the Cloud 9. The place is a particular favorite for surfers as they catch the waves. The sunset view can be a stunning experience for everyone. Cloud 9 is in General Luna which means that all you need to do is to take a tricycle ride worth 30 PHP to get there.

TO TASTE

Harana Surf Resort *Special mission!*

If you've a hankering to try local cuisine, Harana Surf Resort is it. The sound of nature and the crashing waves provide the perfect backdrop music from a plate of Crispy Pata or Pork Legs for 450 PHP to a bowl of Tuna kinilaw doused in milk, chili, and vinegar for 300 PHP.

Lunares Café

If you yearn for sweet energy-spiking foods, the various cheesecake selections in this café will hit the spot. A sweet cup of espresso for 80 PHP is certain to boost up your energy before you hit the waves.

One Hundred Islands

The top tourist attraction that Alaminos City, Pangasinan has is the One Hundred Islands National Park. There are actually 123 islets and islands are tropical paradises that are ready to be explored in a day or an overnight getaway. Here are the top 10 things to know more about the One Hundred Islands before embarking on the trip.

Travel tips

Alaminos City is a 4-5 hour land trip from Manila. If you take the public and air-conditioned bus, the fare would cost around 400 PHP. Alaminos City serves as the gateway to the Hundred Islands. This means that upon arrival in the city you need to take a tricycle ride to Lucap Wharf. Tricycle fare is usually around 80-100 PHP per trip. The tourism office in Lucap Wharf will take care of the island hopping tours. The boat rental fees depend on the size and the itinerary. For instance, hiring a small boat that can accommodate up to 5 people for a day trip will cost around 1,000 PHP. However, if you intend to spend the night in one of the islands, the cost will now be 2,000 PHP.

- Cash payment basis only. Plastic cards do not work here.
- Invest in power banks for your mobile phones or tablets. Charging your gadgets in the charging station is not free.
- Snorkeling gear rental is about 250 PHP

- A bottle of vinegar will be a lifesaver when you get stung by jellyfish while swimming
- Save on tent rentals by bringing your own

Places TO STAY

You have the option to stay overnight on one of the islands or go back to Manila after an island hopping tour for the day. A tent rental for 400 PHP is available for adventurous tourists who want to stay the night in the developed islands. However, if a more comfortable setting is the option, open cottages or cottages with rooms are available. Another option is to stay the night in one of the hotels in Alaminos City.

Natividad Ravara Pension Hotel

If you're a big group of travelers, Natividad Ravara is the hotel to go for. For 500 PHP per head with the location near Lucap Wharf makes it a sweet deal. A functioning kitchen can also be used by the guests if they want to prepare their own food. The marvelous view of the Hundred Islands Park is another plus for this pension house.

Monte Rio Gardens Bed & Breakfast

For the price of 1,800 per night, the Economy Quadruple room with free breakfast is a fantastic deal. Located 300 meters from the center of the city, traveling to Lucap Wharf and back will be convenient and quick.

Governor Island

A Bahay Kubo good for 3 people costs around 1,500 PHP a day in Governor Island, one of the developed islands in the Hundred Islands. An extra drum of water costs 100 PHP and renting a picnic table for the whole day cost 300 PHP.

TO VISIT

Island hopping tours

There are four developed islands in the Hundred Islands: Children's Island, Governor's Island, Quezon Island, and Marcos Island. Kayaking, camping or simply bumming around are the adventures to enjoy while on an island hop tour. A day tour cost about 80 PHP to cover feed from registration (80 PHP), entrance (30 PHP), Environmental (40 PHP), and Insurance (10 PHP). An overnight tour costs 120 PHP. Hiring a motorboat for 1-5 passengers cost 1,400 for an entire day tour. A medium-sized boat cost around 1,800 PHP while a large boat cost about 2,000 PHP. Day tours set no time limits and include island hopping trips to both developed and undeveloped islands. Going back to the wharf to pick up additional food items is free of charge.

Enjoy private time in Bolo Beach

Bolo Beach offers weary travelers a sanctuary from the maddening crowd. This beautiful beach offers talcum-powder white sands, blue sea, and some privacy. The beach is a 19-minute ride away from Alaminos City and is a private haven to tourists that wants to get away from it all. You can take a taxi or a tricycle to reach Bolo Beach. There are boats available for hire of you want to tour the Hundred Islands from there.

Enjoy an instagram time in Governor's Island

The panoramic view provided by Governor's Island is always an instagram moment. Climbing the top of a hill in the island gives an awesome view of the horse-shaped rock formation of the island. The Governor's Island is popular with the locals having been the site where a reality show known as "Big Brother" was entirely filmed during one of their seasons. It is also one of the most developed islands where guests can either tour for the day or stay for the night. Entrance fee is 40 PHP for day tours and 80PHP for night tours. Scuba diving is one of the popular activities to do in Governor's Island.

Cliff-jump at Devil's Island

Cliff jumping off Devil's Island is an activity for the brave and stalwart. The view of beautiful corals and the different kinds of sea creatures are enough rewards for the ones who dare. Making this as one of the stops during an island hopping tour is a must. The jump off point is around 12 feet high and the waters around 6-8 meters deep. You can snorkel your way out of a cave after your jump and head back to shore.

Camping trip in Quezon Island *Special mission!*

Make it a memorable experience by choosing to camp out overnight in one of the developed islands. Camping by the beach is a unique way of enjoying the vacation to the max. Quezon Island offers tent rentals for as little as 400 PHP a night. There's a wealth of activities to take part in Quezon Island. Activities include wall climbing, snorkeling, rappelling, Frisbee, kayaking, and volleyball playing. A restaurant on the second and third floors of the recreation center of the island serves simple food menus that are highly affordable. Added to that is the zipline aerial platform adjacent to the third floor restaurant.

Zipline dare *Special mission!*

Dare to zipline across Quezon Island to Virgin Island. The first zipline is around 393 feet long, costing about $2. The second one is around 1,791 feet, costing about $5-7. A protective headgear and a very secure harness ensure a safe zipline experience for every adventurous tourist who wants to give it a try.

The Calamian Group of Islands

North of Palawan lie the Calamian Group of Islands, now considered as one of the world's most beautiful islands. Lately, the islands have gotten their share of the limelight because of the dive sites and the stunning views. The group of islands that make up the Calamian includes Coron, Busuanga, Calauit, Culion, Banana, and a lot more. Listed below are the 10 tips and guidelines to make you see why the Calamian Islands have to be included in your itinerary.

Travel tips

You can fly from Manila to Busuanga, El Nido or San Jose. The direct flight to these places takes around 40 minutes. Busuanga offers travel tours to Calamian Islands. Island hopping packages for a day cost around 2,047 PHP per person.

Places TO STAY

The Calamian Islands have slowly become a top tourist attraction. This development has also encouraged a burgeoning hotel business. The various islands comprising the Calamian group of islands provide the choice of high-end and budget hotel options for visitors.

Brother Island, El Nido

If you want a private island retreat, the 21,500 PHP resort is the best one there is. This private retreat is the smartest way to enjoy a Calamian vacation if there are more than 6 people in your party.

Bahay Kubo in Busuanga

Inspired by the traditional Filipino home, the Bahay Kubo is a lovely retreat located in Busuanga. Island hopping can be from that point and wreck diving is only a 5-minute boat ride away. For 1,299 PHP a night, staying at Bahay Kubo is a win-win situation.

NVH Vacationhome in Coron

If you prefer to stay in Coron, NVH Vacationhome for 5,305 per night has 3 bedrooms, 2 baths, and the entire home at your disposal. Other amenities include a functioning kitchen with refrigerator, a lounge area, and free WiFi.

TO VISIT

Coron tour

The rock formation that perfectly pairs a barrier reef and a blue lagoon makes Coron one of the outstanding islands, if not the most popular in the Calamian Group of Islands. The popular activities available in Coron include snorkeling, island hopping, food trips or simply watching the beautiful sunset. The only way to enjoy all these is to stay in Coron town. Tour package rates for a Coron Town sightseeing are around 735 PHP per person.

The white sands of Malcapuya Island

A slice of Paradise setting of white and glistening sands, swaying palms, and clear turquoise waters awaits every visitor in the island of Malcapuya. The island holds the distinguished reputation of having the longest and whitest sand beach among the Calamian group of Islands. Since it can only be reached through an island hopping tour, the place has remained pristine and well-preserved. Snorkeling and swimming are allowed during a stop in the islands. Camping overnight is also allowed. The way to do it is to hire an overnight boat trip, tent, and guide. Rates vary with the season. You can ask more information about rates in Coron.

The lush vegetation of Kayangan Lake

Kayangan Lake is part of Coron. The stunning views offered by the lake surrounded by limestone walls and crystal clear waters are must-sees in the Calamian tour. If you are staying in Coron, Kayangan Lake is a tricycle ride away. If you choose to go for a swim, a small wooden platform and walkway can hold your things. However, Kayangan is a famous tourist spot so don't expect the place to be quite and private. The lagoon serves as the parking space for bangkas disgorging their boat tour passengers.

Sea Cow Watching in Coron *Special mission!*

Coron offers a unique ecotourism activity which is sea cow watching. The sea cows are gentle creatures, mainly subsisting on sea grass communities. Booking a diving trip to watch the Dugong cost around 2,000 PHP. However, the rate varies with certified and non-certified divers. It is best to read people reviews about the different diving centers before you choose the one to book.

Experience Calauit Safari Park

Choosing the Busuanga island hopping tour will take you to Calauit Safari Park. This unique park features giraffes, impalas, elands, gazelles, zebras, and more roaming freely over the area. A group tour from Coron is the best option to get there. The cost is around 2500 PHP per head. For a group of 4 people, hiring a private boat for 7500 PHP can be a sweet deal since the tour includes some islands such as the beautiful Black Island. Entrance fee is 400 PHP for foreigners and 200 PHP for Filipinos. A land rover for 1000 PHP is another option to take for a land trip to Calauit.

Snorkeling at North Cay Island

The pure white sands and the blue clear waters of this small island make it a perfect site for snorkeling activities. The great variety of tropical fishes presents an added excitement to the island hopping tour. Another option is to go for a Calauit Safari and North Cay snorkeling package for 3000 PHP per head. This way, you get to see and experience two iconic places in the Calamian group of Islands in an inexpensive way.

Take time to visit historical sites

Culion Island, a part of the Calamian Islands used to be the biggest leprosarium in the country and the world. The WHO has declared it leprosy-free in 2006, making it a great island to explore historical sites such as the centuries-old La Immaculada Concepcion Church. A boat charter to Culion Island from Coron cost around 3500 PHP. Coron offers half day tours for 1000 PHP per head. Included historical and tourist spots are St.

Augustine Church, Maquinit Hotspring, Town Plaza, Mt. Tapyas View Deck, Cashew Harvest, Lualhati Park, the Public Market, and the Souvenir Shops.

TO TASTE

Take a food trip down Coron Town by discovering the fresh seafood offerings. Mingling with the natives is the best way to learn more about Coron and the Calamian Group of Islands. Here are the restaurants reputed to provide the best local cuisine in Coron:

1. Tita Eash Eatery
2. Big Mama's Pinoy Hot Pot and Grill
3. Lolo Nonoy's Food Station
4. Bistro Coron
5. Kawayanan Grill

Gigantes Group of Islands, Panay

Off the coast of Carles town in Panay Island is a group of islands known as the Islas de Gigantes. Gigantes Sur and Gigantes Norte are the largest of these islands. 'Gigante" is the Spanish term for giant and the islands were renamed when supposedly giant bones were unearthed in one of the caves. Resorts are found on both these big islands or you can opt to stay in the town of Carles. Here are ten tips to make the visit to Panay fun and exciting.

Travel tips

It costs 3,457 to fly from Manila to Roxas City. The 2-3 hours land trip from Roxas to Carles cost around 197.00 PHP. A 2-hour ferry boat ride from Carles port will take you to the Gigantes. The faster way is through From Roxas City to either Estancia or Carles.

- Food items and other necessities are better purchased at Estancia. Carles is a very small town featuring only tiny stores.
- Freshly-caught seafood can be bought only in the early hours of the morning.
- Make sure of a steady supply of drinking water during your stay in the Gigantes.
- Some resorts in Carles may not have their own generators. A resort that does not have one relies on a scheduled electricity supply which is turned on during late afternoons up to 11 PM.

Places TO STAY

Red Mandarin Beach Resort in Carles

Budget tour packages are fast becoming the norm in the Gigantes. A package costing 1,699 PHP covers a 2-day tour and an overnight stay. The one-night stay included in the package is in Red Mandarin Beach Resort in Carles. The rooms in the resort are quite large and cost 1,000 PHP per head if you go for the air-conditioned rooms. The budget package only covers a fan room and shared bathrooms.

Entire Apartment in Estancia

Estancia also overlooks the Gigantes with chartered boats to go around the islands. For 704 a night, an entire floor in the apartment is at your disposal. For 704/night you may opt for the first or third floor of the apartment. Each floor has 2 bedrooms, a bathroom, and a functional kitchen. The 2nd floor is occupied by the owner.

Jaja's Garden in Carles

Staying at this quite expensive resort gives you a beautiful garden and a private beachfront. Priced at 8,012/night, you have the choice of having a huge air-conditioned room good for 4 people or a private air-conditioned room for 2 people.

TO VISIT

Island hopping tours

Island hopping remains the most popular activity in the Gigantes. Indulging in this activity provides scenic views and various activities in both Gigantes Norte and Sur.

Budget tour packages are the popular choices among the visitors for the low cost. The only downside is the fan rooms and shared bathrooms for the included overnight stay. However, upgrading to an air-conditioned room with private bath can be arranged.

The budget package island hopping tours include all meals. This is a sweet deal for the food provided is almost unlimited. You can eat your fill of fresh delicacies such as crabs, grilled fish, squid, and scallops. Snacks are not included so bring your own. Coffee and chocolate drinks are unlimited as well. Environmental and entrance fees to the different islands are included in the budget package tour.

Hiring a private Bangka including a guide costs 2,500 PHP. Added expenses are food and entrance and environmental fees in each island.

The iconic lighthouse and cave spelunking in Gigantes Norte

This functioning lighthouse in Gigantes Norte is already centuries old. Standing 39 feet high, it was built during the Spanish era. The tower of the lighthouse is now solar-powered, serving as the beacon for ships passing in the night. A round-trip tricycle ride costing around 60 PHP per person is your way of reaching the lighthouse from the place where the chartered boat is docked. Exploring the Bakwitan Caves is a must for cave spelunkers. A round-trip tricycle ride costing around 200 PHP per head is the only means of transport. A guide costs an additional 500 PHP.

Dipping in Tangke Saltwater Lagoon

Tangke Saltwater Lagoon is located in Gigantes Sur and very similar to the one in Palawan. The clear waters surrounded by rock formations are stunning to say the least. The natural saltwater pool found behind the rock cliffs of Gigantes Sur offers a stunning view and a refreshing swim to all travelers. Going there is usually included in the island hopping tours in the Gigantes. Entrance fee is around 20 PHP per head.

Include Cabugao Gamay Island in your itinerary

One of the smaller islands of the Gigantes is Cabugao Island. The unique shape of the island can be photographed at a certain vantage point. Sunbathing and swimming on the pristine white sand beach are the usual activities to indulge in. Cabugao is again part of the island hopping tour. Entrance fee is about 70 PHP per head.

Rock climbing in Gigantes Sur *Special mission!*

The sheer rock formations surrounding Gigantes Sur make it the perfect spot for rock climbers. The cliffs have also encouraged diving activities. This activity can be included in a boat hopping tour to Gigantes Sur. Entrance fee is 20 PHP per head.

Marvel at the sandbar of Bantigue Island

Bantigue Island may be one of the smallest islands of the Gigantes group of islands but it boasts of the longest sandbar. Plan the visit to coincide with low tide so you can run through its entire length. There is no entrance fee but renting a table cost 50 PHP. A thriving scallops business is alive in the island. Purchasing a minimum order of about 100 PHP includes cooking the scallops for you. Expect to be surprised at the disappearance of the sandbar in the afternoons.

TO TASTE

The Gigantes is dubbed the scallop capital of the country, making it doubly important to try them. You can buy them directly from fishermen and have them cooked any way you want it at nearby restaurants for a small charge. Scallops usually cost around 1 PHP per shell and buying them in bulk is the only way to enjoy them. Other fresh seafood offerings in Carles include crabs, fish, and squid.

Carles does not have any restaurants. It is only in neighboring towns such as Estancia that you get to eat in restaurants.

Caramoan Peninsula

Caramoan Peninsula is an under-the-radar tourist destination in the Philippines. The place is a serene, quiet, and beautiful paradise of lush jungles, wonderful cities, and stunning beaches. The peninsula became highlighted when the TV show Survivor took place here. Here are top ten guidelines to make the visit relaxing, soothing, and enjoyable.

Travel tips

You can take a direct 45 minute flight from Manila to Naga. Round trip fares cost around 4,337 PHP. From Naga Airport, an air-conditioned van to Sabang Port cost around 150 PHP per head. A 1 hour and 45 minute boat ride costing 120 PHP takes you to Caramoan Guijalo Port. Special trips to Caramoan from Sabang Port cost about 3000 PHP.

- Always include a first aid kit in your things especially if you intend to spend a night in one of the islands.
- Pack adequate food such as snacks to tide you over during boat tours. Some islands may not provide food. Your boatman can be the best person to ask about the food conditions in the various islands.
- Protect your things. Bring loads of Ziploc bags to protect gadgets and money.
- Clean as you go. Protect the environment by leaving no trace of waste on every island you travel.

Places to Stay

There are plenty of resorts in Caramoan to choose from. Read reviews of the various resorts online as a way to get the best ones offered. Top-rated places to stay in Caramoan include:

Casita Mia Bed and Breakfast

The Casita Mia Bed and Breakfast is a beautiful hotel that offers all the amenities. The free breakfast is an added plus to the hotel. Rates start at 1,500 PHP a night.

West Peninsula Villas

Rates starting at 1,500 PHP per day give you a luxurious room and free use of a lovely pool.

La Casa Roa

For budget conscious travelers, La Casa Roa provides a homey atmosphere. It is clean and the price rate of 750 PHP per day is the best there is.

TO VISIT

Beach hopping in Caramoan

Other tourist destinations in the Philippines usually have island hopping. It is only in Caramoan that the activity is beach hopping. There are two beach hopping packages to choose from. One package costing around 1000-1500 PHP includes beaches of Gota, Matukad, Lahus, and Hunongan. The other package costing around 2000-3000 PHP includes hopping to more distant beaches such as Sabitang Laya, Manlawi Sandbar, and Cotivas Island.

Some of the islands cannot be explored as they are under contract with the Survivor TV series. These islands will only become available for exploring and visiting in 2033 yet if Survivor will not extend their lease contract.

Rock climbing in Matukad Island

The sharp rock formations of Matukad Island pose a challenge to any rock climber enthusiast. Another must-see in the island is the incredible of a huge milkfish in the enchanted lagoon. However, the island's selling point is the powdery white sand that can definitely compete with Boracay. Chartering a boat to make a special trip to Matukad Island costs around 2000-3000 PHP.

Marvel at the Lady of Peace Grotto

The Caglago Mountain in Caramoan houses this humongous 26-foot image of the Virgin Mary. It is said to be the largest in the country, acting as a lighthouse when it is all lit up at night. A tricycle ride to the place cost around 50PHP. The challenge to each tourist is the climb of 557 steps to the top.

Include Cotivas Island in the itinerary

Cotivas Island is another paradise destiny when on a boat tour in Caramoan. Entrance fee is 50 PHP per head and renting a hut to eat lunch costs 100 PHP. Cold sodas can be bought along with ice from the natives for around 100 PHP. The long stretch of white sands, the clear waters, and the swaying palm trees are the attractions provided by the island.

Treasure-hunting in Manipis Cave

The cave is reputed to hide the famous General Yamashita treasure. You may be the lucky one to discover the amassed treasure trove left behind by the general during WWII. Manipis Cave can be made a part of the beach tour itinerary.

Be a "survivor" by staying in the West Peninsula Villas *Special mission!*

Caramoan was the setting of one Survivor series. The West Peninsula Villas offer visitors the chance to experience being a member of the Survivor series. Room rates start from 1442 PHP a night with free breakfast. It served as a peaceful haven for the Survivor contestants during the filming of the series.

TO TASTE

Fresh and affordable are the main characteristics of every dining experience in Caramoan. The restaurants may not be fancy, but the foods they serve are guaranteed fresh and delicious. Here are the top restaurant picks in Caramoan:

Island View Lodge and Restobar

The all-Filipino cuisine served in this restaurant includes the popular Bicol Express, a super spicy pork concoction. Eating for one can cost 400 PHP.

Caramotan Grill and Restobar

International, Filipino, and other Asian delicacies are served in this restaurant. Their grilled fresh squid is to die for.

Wowoys Seafood Restaurant *Special mission!*

Fresh seafood and Filipino food are the specialties of the house. They have a "secret menu" dare daily that will challenge every palate. Lone dining can cost around 280 PHP.

Caramoan Bed and Dine

The Bicol Express and Chopsuey are the restaurant's specialties. They also serve a variety of fresh seafood and Filipino dishes.

Bay Sand Food Stop

Filipino and fresh seafood are the things expected from this restaurant. Open from 7AM to 10PM, this restaurant has your back at any time.

Mindoro

Mindoro is an island that is sandwiched between Palawan and Luzon islands. It is a dream island for hikers, food connoisseurs, backpackers, divers, and beach bums. The local cuisine consists of healthy doses of veggies and fruits as well as the freshest seafood. Read our top ten tips for a memorable Mindoro visit.

Travel tips

There's a direct 30-minute flight 3 times a day from Manila to San Jose, Mindoro costing around 3,315 PHP per person. A cheaper option is to take a bus ride from Manila to the bus ferry to Mindoro. It may take a longer time travel but only costs around 1,037 to 1,459 PHP per person.

- Corals are not to be stepped on.
- Aqua shoes are a must when you want to access snorkeling sites
- Carry cash. There are only 3 ATM machines in the town proper and transactions are always on cash basis.

Places TO STAY

Mindoro is already a popular tourist destination which means that there is no lack of accommodations. Choose the one that fits your budget and enjoy your stay. Puerto Galera is synonymous to Mindoro and also the best place to stay in.

Sunny Beach Resort

One of the popular resorts to stay in is the Sunny Beach Resort. Its close proximity to the town and other tourist spots make it an ideal hotel. Notwithstanding, the price rate of 2500 PHP is a good deal for this 3-star hotel that includes free breakfast. Seasonal discounts can lower the price to as low as 450 PHP a night.

Steps Garden Resort *Special mission!*

If you prefer a more swanky setting, Steps Garden Resort with a pool and excellent location is the best option. For 1,550 PHP a night and free breakfast for two, it's a sweet deal altogether.

Coco Beach Island Resort

The resort is quite popular with foreign visitors who want the best vacation experience in Mindoro. It can be an expensive choice at room rates start at 9,300 PHP per day. However, season discounts can lower it to 3,334 PHP per day while you enjoy all the amenities and luxuries of the resort. Free breakfast is served throughout your stay.

TO VISIT

Puerto Galera experience

If you like the party vibe, Puerto Galera offers that kind of ambiance and more. The white sand beach and the crystal clear blue waters add more allure to the place as well as the entertainment it provides. The Puerto Galera scene matches that of Boracay and staying within the proximity offers the best of both worlds: a party scene and a private hideaway to get away from it all.

Scuba diving in Sabang Beach

Other than the vibrant night life, Sabang Beach is the best diving spot. Some of the exotic marine species you'll be able to see in a diving trip include Blue Mandarin fish, Blue Ringed Octopus, and lush coral reefs. Mindoro is considered as the country's diving place which has encouraged diving resorts to come up with package deals to include stay and diving lessons.

Cool and refreshing Tukuran Falls

Off-the-beaten track Tukuran Falls is the ideal place to cool down and enjoy the view after a long trip. You have the option to rent a motorbike, ride in a jeepney, hire a private van or hire a tricycle to get to the place. A jeep or multi-cab tour costs around 2000 PHP good for 8 people. The falls is an under-the-radar attraction that is still as enchanting as the well-known ones.

Tamaraw Falls *Special mission!*

The most famous falls in Puerto Galera is the Tamaraw Falls. The place is an hour and 45 minutes trip from Puerto Galera and chartering a jeepney tour is the best way to enjoy it. Going for the Inland jeepney tour package for 1,500 PHP per head includes Virgin Beach and the Tamaraw Falls.

Island hopping tours

1,500 PHP is the standard rate for an 8-person island hopping boat tour. The tour includes sightseeing, snorkeling, and swimming activities in Sandbar Island, Coral Garden, Bayanan Beach, and Haligi Beach.

Snorkeling in Coral Garden

A boat tour can take you to Coral Garden beach where snorkeling is the main activity. The snorkeling site however, cannot be accessed by a standard-sized boat. This means that you have to rent a small boat on site for an extra charge of 200 PHP per person to reach the snorkeling site.

TO TASTE

Puerto Galera is often referred to as the "poor man's Boracay" which means that food is less expensive as well.

Big Apple

The restaurant offers western food such as the Rib Eye Steak with your choice of rice, sweet corn, baked potato or French fries for 450 PHP. Their pizza version called Big Apple's Diver Pizza for 320 PHP is highly recommended.

Full Moon *special mission!*

Fast service, delicious food, and affordable prices are the things offered in Full Moon. Their Spicy Seafood Hotpot and Australian-Style Rump Steak are the specialties of the house.

Club Mabuhay

A taste of Filipino cooking such as fresh grilled seafood can be enjoyed at Club Mabuhay. The restaurant also serves international cuisines and their Spaghetti with Meatballs is a must-try.

Made in the USA
Las Vegas, NV
20 August 2024

94135521R00033